Gardening Master Guide!

Learn Step By Step How To Use Companion Plants For A Successful Flower Or Vegetable Garden

Copyright

TABLE OF CONTENT

Introduction

I want to thank you and congratulate you for downloading the book, *"Gardening For Beginners Master Guide! Learn Step By Step How To Use Companion Plants For A Successful Flower Or Vegetable Garden"*.

This book has actionable steps and strategies on how to raise a successful flower or vegetable garden using companion gardening.

What makes for a beautiful and healthy garden? If you ask the layman, they will probably answer along the lines of organic manure injection and elimination of pests and put a full stop to it. When you ask any seasoned gardener, they will tell you that one of the most overlooked tips is that of having a diverse mix of plants in your yard.

Many of them too, even the ones with the most scientific of orientations, will confess of a deep rooted belief that certain combinations of plants have extraordinary powers for aiding one another grow. If any of this sounds a little farfetched, it might serve you well to understand that scientific research has unearthed just as much. Well, this is what has come to be referred to as companion gardening. So, what is companion planting gardening? Why opt for it? We shall cover all that in this book. I will also give you a step-by-step formula on successful companion gardening.

Thanks again for downloading this book, I hope you enjoy it!

The Concept of Companion Gardening

Many plants have natural substances present in the leaves, roots, flowers, and other plant parts that have the capacity to repel or even attract insects. In some situations too, some plants have the capacity to enhance the rate of growth of other plant varieties. Actually, time-tested gardening experts agree that when certain types of plants are made to grow together, they become "helpmates". This simply means that plants, just like human beings, need good companions to thrive.

As a gardener, you can use this to your advantage in one way or the other depending on what you are looking for. This makes it important to ponder on building good and effective plant communities when you are planting your garden especially given the fact that this is the most important concept in all of companion planting gardening.

Survival for the fittest Vs companion planting

Except for the processes of fruiting and growth, plants are pretty much idle objects. They are rooted to a solitary spot all their lives and have very little control over the environment.

Survival for the fittest

These two traits will generally work against the plant's growth and survival, especially when you consider that nature's top stipulation is that resources must be fought for. Science has confirmed that indeed, some plants "bully" other plant varieties. Certain plants will be characterized by rapid growth, crowding other plants and taking up more water and nutrients. Some are adapted to release toxins into the soil, which will then retard plant growth or simply just kill them off. A common example is the Black Walnut tree that releases hydrojuglone into the soil.

Companion gardening

Other plants, on the other hand, are "upstanding" and good companions. These plants inject nutrients into the soil, drawing the beneficial insect types to the garden. Similarly, they may also confuse insects in the search of host plants. This is what companion planting is all about: rather than a protracted "war" for resources that will see plant quality take a hit, companion planting will establish a fabric of supplementation and growth complementation.

As a gardener, it would not be wrong to view yourself as the city planner and mayor of that city that is your garden. By growing plants with beneficial companions, you inspire prosperity and health in your little city.

How companion planting works in pest control

Have you come across Integrated Pest Management? If you have heard about it, you should definitely know that the very use of companion planting is a vital part of this. How is this? In essence, opting for companion planting will aid in bringing about a balanced eco-system to the landscape, thus giving nature the necessary tools to take care of itself and carry out its job.

Here is how nature works: nature will integrate a diverse range of plant life, animals, insects and other organisms of the world into each ecosystem in such a way and form that there is zero waste. The death of organism X will mean food for organism Y, translating to symbolic relationships all round. As such, due to the multiple intricate ways it works with nature and the ecology, it is not a rare thing to hear companion planting labeled as a "holistic concept".

By using this type of gardening, gardeners will discover that discouraging harmful pests becomes an easier task, and this is without losing those allies that prove beneficial in gardening. Multiple herbs and flowers that are usable as companion plants are present. In as much as this book will guide you on the best ones to use and what to pair together, feel free to experiment and find out what works in your particular gardening yard.

Achieving Functional Beauty

Companion planting will combine beauty with purpose to give you the healthiest environment you could ask for your plants. Above all, you must remember to have fun with your plants and let your imagination soar. With gardening, combinations of plants that complement each other's growth has not been exhausted yet.

How Companion Planting works: Tips for the novice

As in the planning of a city, the way that you lay your garden out is extremely crucial. By all means, do not grow your vegetables in large sized patches or in lengthy rows. Rather, keep it all controlled as you interplant. Having large groups of the same kind of plant without the interjection of companion planting will only serve as a beacon to problematic pests.

If you set out your garden so that the mix of herbs with your veggies is thorough, it becomes really hard for insects to find your plants. The scent of the herbs and flowers, as well as the visible change-up in color has been believed to genuinely confuse pests.

Certain flowers and herbs will also serve as attractants to pests that are beneficial.

99% of all sensible articles on the subject of companion planting reference "Three sister planting". What is this? It is an age-old grouping system that involves the growing of beans, corn and squash (often pumpkins) in one area. As the stalks of corn grow upward, the beans you have planted alongside find a natural support on the stalks. Beans, just like every legume out there, fix nitrogen into the soil, which then serves to support the sizable nutritional needs that characterize corn. Squash grows very fast, and their large leaves shade out weeds, acting as a natural block for the same.

It is highly recommended that you adopt the three sister planting system of companion planting. Not only has it been workable for generations, it also further drives the point home that good plant companions support one another.

Why Opt For Companion Planting Gardening?

While most gardeners have heard of companion planting and the benefits attached to the practice, many are still confused by what companion planting is and especially how the principles of the practice can be applied while gardening.

The benefits highlighted will not only attempt to show the massive upside of companion planting, but also outlay the principles of the same.

Companion plants will attract beneficial insects

Planting a mix of herbs and flowers among fruit trees and veggies serves to encourage a healthy diversity of living organisms to move into your garden. Plants that attract insects that will grow readily from the seed level will include herbs like sage, thyme, coriander, mint and chives, as well as flowers such as calendula, cosmos, Echinacea, lavender, and marigold.

Phacelia, a member of the Yates seed range, is often very successful at attracting insects that will benefit the garden, such as honeybees (which are valuable agents of pollination) and hoverflies (which predate on aphids).

Companion plants play a masking role and act as decoy plants

Masking plants are plants that will emit an odor that will disguise the smell of the desirable plant species, confusing the pests that would otherwise attack them.

A classic example is planting onions, chives or garlic in close proximity to roses so as to deter aphids, thrips and other pests that prey on them.

Decoy plants are close relatives of masking plants. The decoy plants, rather than confuse the insects with the weapon of scent, will draw the pests to them and away from the other plants. Nasturtium is perhaps the best known decoy plant to gardeners. These plants acts as pest magnets, drawing pests away from the other plants and onto themselves.

In case you have never heard of the term decoy plants but have come across the term martyr plants, they all refer to the same thing. The term "martyr plants" comes from the reasoning that these plants are prepared to "suffer" so that the other plant species can be safe.

Companion plants will play the role of nurturing plants

There are companion plants that will play the role of improving the surrounding conditions of their neighbors. The very best examples are beans, peas and other varied members of the legume family. Why is this? These plants are blessed with the wonderful gift of being able to draw nitrogen from the atmosphere and fixing it in the soil. When you plant plants close to peas and other legumes, they will benefit from that nitrogen that has been fixed into the soil by the legumes.

Companion planting will support plant diversity

This is beneficial to the farmer and the ecosystem. It is also beneficial to the soil, as it serves as a feeding source to the variety of the environment. Plant diversity will directly lead to insect diversity, which seems to have the effect of cutting down the number of pests and loading on the number of beneficial insects in the garden.

What Do You Grow With Companion Planting? Top Vegetables, Flowers, Natural Repellents And Herbs That Function Best In Companion Gardening
Part I: Top herbs to help your garden thrive

Companion planting gardening is a very efficient natural way of offering your garden protection from pests as well as promoting healthy growth in all the veggies, herbs, and flowers in your garden. Some plants greatly benefit the soil too, fixing nitrogen in it and elevating its fertility. Other plants repel specific diseases and pests or enhance the flavor of vegetables and fruits.

Herbs particularly stand out in the trap-planting context, as they can play the dual role of repelling pests and attracting beneficial insects at the same time. Bees, ladybugs, and butterflies are some of the insects herbs can attract to your garden.

Here are some of the top herbs to employ in companion planting, along with some traditional wisdom to get you up and running.

Basil

Basil greatly benefits the healthy growth of petunia plants and aids in improving the flavor of tomatoes, peppers, asparagus, and oregano. However, you must not plant basil near sage or common rue, as the quality of these will only plummet. If you are planting basil as the main plant, usually to harvest its potent essential oil, you can increase the essential oils by planting anise or chamomile beside it.

Chamomile

Chamomile is an excellent plant to plant besides other herbs to increase the essential oils in them. In addition, this herb has been known to help wheat, onions, basil, cucumber and cabbage plants thrive in the garden. This potent herb also serves to attract wasps and hoverflies, which greatly assist in pollination while feeding on various pest insects like aphids.

Borage

This herb acts as a potent deterrent to cabbageworms and tomato hornworms. Additionally, it improves the composition of the soil while assisting the plant it is planted next to attain better resilience and resistance to pests and diseases. For superb results, plant your borage along with tomatoes, strawberries, and squash. Not only will the flavor be vastly improved, the amount of fruit that you harvest will show a considerable increase in number.

Dill

Dill herb makes for an excellent companion to cabbage, lettuce, sweet corn, onions, and cucumbers. While a potent herb and an excellent companion herb, keep it away from carrots, lavender, tomatoes and caraway by all means. This herb will check the aphids, squash bugs, and spider mites in your garden by acting as a repellent to them and will attract honeybees, wasps, and hoverflies. To provide the phenomenon of cross pollination, keep dill away from fennel.

Garlic

Garlic, as you may well know by now, has a vast haul of health benefits tagged to it. In addition to these, it keeps the likes of rabbits and tree borers away from your garden, as well as cabbage loopers, aphids, codling moths, snails, Japanese beetles, ants, carrot root flies, and cabbage maggots. Its true powers in companion planting show when it is planted along with apple, peach and pear trees, cucumbers, roses, peas, celery and lettuce.

Part II: Pairing Plants that are mutually beneficial to one another: Vegetables, Flowers and other natural repellents for pests

Vegetables

What are some of the top vegetables that truly have their best brought out of them when paired with others, and what exactly do you pair them with? Read on to be enlightened.

Radishes

Radishes are common and are to be easily found in multiple gardens. Radishes give phenomenal yields when grown with the right companion plants. One vegetable that helps them thrive when grown along with radishes is the lettuce. The natural, consistent leafiness of the lettuce plant provides perpetual mulch for the soil that both of these plants will benefit from, as the leaves of the lettuce plants fall. Lettuce leaves will also act as pest deterrent and provide much needed shade for radishes as they grow.

Other great companion plants for the radish include chervil, squash, and cucumber. Chervils play the role of increasing the growth rate of radishes as well as the taste. Radishes will repel the squash borers' larvae that carve holes in the root systems of the squash plants. Keep radishes away from cabbage plants, turnips, cauliflower and Brussels plants. Radishes and spinach plants make for a good team, as the radish leaves attract mining pests, sparing the spinach roots.

Broccoli

This vegetable serves as a great companion plant to multiple kinds of beans, coriander, beets, borage, marjoram, tomatoes, and cucumbers.

Flowers

Marigolds

If you are looking for a great flower to keep around your veggie garden, you cannot go wrong with the marigold flower. They are known to act as repellents to pests such as the Mexican bean beetle. French marigolds will emit a substance on the immediate area that they grow in, and this scent will kill nematodes. When grown with tomatoes, they will protect them by keeping away whiteflies. The Mexican marigolds are regarded as some of the most powerful repellents of insects and they effectively stunt the growth of blind weeds in the immediate area that they are grown in. However, keep marigolds away from cabbage and beans, as they may act as an herbicide to these.

Geraniums

These are perennial flowers. They do well to help corn, roses, grapes and peppers by attracting pests to them while repelling leafhoppers. Do not plant these next to tomato plants however.

Petunias

These flowers are very similar to geraniums. They will repel pests like leafhoppers while attracting others to them, so that the other plants are not affected. They are known to repel aphids, Japanese beetles, and asparagus beetles.

Natural pest repellents

Ants

The most effective repellents for ants are catmint, mint, spearmint and garlic

Mildew

To starve off mildew, plant dried sage, chives and nettle along with your vegetables

Moths

To keep moths away from your garden, the plants to grow are mint, sage, thyme, pennyroyal, rosemary, lavender, and wormwood, along with your vegetables.

Cabbage butterflies

To keep away cabbage butterflies, you will need to plant sage, rosemary, mint, garlic, dill, tansy, oregano, and chamomile.

Part III: Pairs and Combinations: Winning Combinations that never flop

What are some of the finest combinations that you can never go wrong with?

Chives and Roses

In case you do not know, gardeners have been in the practice of planting garlic along with rose for ages now. Why is this? Garlic is very potent as a repellant for pests that prey on roses. Garlic chives most probably have the same repelling capacity. Additionally, their tiny purple/ white flowers look amazing with rose flowers when late spring arrives.

Cabbage and Tomatoes

Tomatoes are great repellents for diamondback moth larvae that are basically caterpillars that chew large holes in the leaves of cabbage plants. This has an overwhelmingly positive impact on cabbage plants, as they can grow and make food for themselves with their leaves untouched and whole.

Cucumbers and Nasturtiums

The nasturtiums, with their vining stems, make them superb companions to your cucumbers as they grow. They are also great to grow with squash plants. Nasturtiums excellently repel cucumber beetles, but the real upside to them is that the farmer can rely on them as a habitat for predatory insects, such as ground beetles and spiders.

Pigweed or ragweed and peppers

It has been discovered that 9 times out of 10, leafminers will prefer weeds to pepper plants. The tip here is to be very careful to remove the flowers of the weeds before they can set seed. If you bypass this step, you are going to have a very hard time controlling the weeds in your garden.

Cabbage and Dill

Dill makes for a superb companion for cabbage family plants. Several examples will include Brussels sprouts and broccoli. In turn, the cabbages will offer support to the floppy dill plant. The Dill plant will attract tiny beneficial wasps that will then prey on imported cabbageworms along with other pests that affect the cabbage plant.

Corn and beans

The beans will serve as attractants to beneficial insects that will prey on pests of corn. This is with the examples of fall armyworms, leafhoppers, and leaf beetles. In turn, the corn will provide excellent stilts for the bean vines to climb up with.

Lettuce and tall flowers

Cleome (spider flower) and Nicotiana (flowering tobacco) will give the lettuce plant the kind of light shade that it thrives in.

Radishes and Spinach

When you plant radishes among your spinach plants, they will attract leafminers to them, and away from the spinach plant. The damage that the leafminers will inflict on the radishes will in no way prevent the radishes from thriving underground.

Sweet asylum and potatoes

The sweet asylum has small-sized flowers that serve to attract beneficial insects, with the example of predatory wasps. Plant the sweet asylum plant along with bushy crops like the potato, or simply let it spread to form a ground cover under plants that arch, like the broccoli.

The sweet asylum comes with its own bonus: the sweet fragrance it produces will scent your garden all summer long.

Dwarf zinnias and Cauliflower

The nectar that the dwarf zinnias produce will lure ladybugs and other pests and insects that will help protect your cauliflower patch by preying on pests that destroy it.

Catnip and Collards

It has been found out by studies that when you plant catnip along with collards, the effect is that flea-beetle damage on the collards is greatly checked.

Love-in-a-mist and Strawberries

Love-in-a-mist is tall and grows lovely blue flowers. It looks truly wonderful when it is grown in the center of a wide-sized row of strawberry plants.

Melons and marigolds

Certain varieties of marigolds serve to control nematodes in the melon roots with the same effectiveness shown by chemical treatments.

Pooled combinations that work superbly

*Grow your tomatoes along with French marigolds. The marigolds will emit a powerful odor that will repel the black fly and the green fly.

*Grow your carrots and plants in the cabbage family with sage, as this helps ward off the pests that afflict them. Both are characterized by strong scents that work to drive each other's pests away.

*Plant your nasturtiums with cabbage plants. The former are a powerful magnet for caterpillars, which will then move to the nasturtium and leave the cabbage plants alone to grow and thrive.

*When you plant garlic among your rose plants, aphids will find it hard to prey on the roses, as the garlic will ward them off.

*Plant leeks and carrots together on the allotment you have set aside for your vegetable plants to shield them against a good number of harmful pests. Leeks will repel the carrot fly and the carrots will ward off the onion flies and leek moths.

Watering Systems: How Do You Set These Up For This Type Of Gardening To Improve Conservation?

Smart techniques to incorporate to conserve water without leaving the plants in your companion gardening project thirsty as you set up your watering system

As a smart companion plant gardener, you need to understand that watering systems that are wasteful (including sprinkler systems) might have worked in centuries ago but not today. Here are some watering tips that will strike a lovely balance between sufficient watering and conservation.

#Hand check

Before you brandish your watering can, check the soil moisture in your garden using the handiest natural tool in the world i.e. your finger. Push your finger into the soil, especially the soil around your plants. What you want is for the top couple of inches or so to be dry but the soil underneath that to be moist. The other thing is to keep up to speed with weather forecasting reports to see if there is any rain forthcoming. This may help you conserve water you may otherwise have used up.

#Understand that timing is everything

In hot weather, make sure to water your garden in the morning to give your plants enough time to take up water before strong winds and the full sun impose themselves on the moisture. This will also protect your companion gardening project from sporting wilted plants in the afternoon. In times of prolonged drought, keep your plants covered with a shade cloth to limit transpiration. This applies mainly to those plants you consider delicate and sensitive. If you cannot do your watering in the morning, try late afternoon but not too late. The foliage should have enough time to dry off, otherwise the plants risk being prone to fungal diseases.

#Keep your watering deep and infrequent

Seedlings and seeds will usually demand for water to be close to the surface. However for the more established plants, deep watering is required so that the plants may develop a root system of finding water in the subsoil when drought comes around. However, be careful so as not to overwater your plants. You want soil that is damp but in no way soggy, down to around six inches below the surface. In waterlogged soils, the roots become oxygen-deprived and may well lose the capacity to take up water because of this.

#Plant your thirsty plants in one place and repeat the same thing with the tough plants

Some plants in your garden will require less water than others will given that different plants have different water requirements. Try your best to pair those plants that use up the same amount of water together. Do all you can to zone your plantings according to the water needs. If you have soil that holds water naturally and yet is not enough for all your plantings, use it for the thirsty plants, like lettuce. You should also know that while basil is an excellent herb to use as a companion plant, it is a "thirsty" plant i.e. takes up a lot of water. As such, you should ideally plant basil along with lettuce plants.

#Mulch your crops

The advantage with mulching is that it insulates the soil. This helps the soil conserve its moisture as well as keep it weed free. You should remember that weeds are the primary suckers of the soil's moisture.

With the types of plants we are dealing with here, soil-feeding mulches done in the short term will work best (for example, pea straw). The mulch is able to last until the time to rotate your crop comes by. The mulch remains can then be dug in to improve the structure of the soil.

Harvesting And Dealing Effectively With Weeds And Problems Facing The Crops

Harvesting radishes

You can harvest some radish varieties in as little as 3 weeks especially in summer. However, ensure that the radishes don't stay in the ground for far too long after maturity since they often tend to deteriorate pretty fast.

To harvest, cut the tops off then wash them before drying them. You can then store them in plastic bags in a refrigerator. As for radish greens, you can store them for about 3 weeks.

Harvesting basil

After your seedlings have hit their first six leaves, you can start pruning from the second set. This is often just when the plant starts to bud and right before its flowers start blooming. When the branch gets 6-8 leaves, you can prune again (this time, ensure you prune the first set of leaves). Actually, if you commit to pruning your basils regularly, 12 plants of basil is enough to supply you with about 4-6 cups of basil leaves weekly.

After harvesting, ensure to store the leaves under refrigeration since this has been proven to prevent the leaves from losing their flavor. Before freezing, dry the basil sprigs first then pack them in airtight plastic bags.

Harvesting Dill

How do you go about harvesting dill?

-Gently set about harvesting your herbs using a pair of sharp pruning scissors. This is especially vital if the plan is to store dill in your refrigerator or you plan on heating or air-drying it. Damage inflicted on the leaves will only lead to discolored leaves and a higher susceptibility to decay.

-Harvest leaves just before the dill flowers open. The day before you harvest them, spray the dill leaves with water to ensure that they are clean when you pick them. Pick your dill early in the morning. If this is impossible, dip the stems in water for about 2 hours.

-Strip off any damaged lower leaves and be sure to remove any flower heads present.

-Use a rubber band or kitchen string to combine your dill stems loosely into small bundles. Do not bunch your herbs tightly as this only encourages the growth of mold, as they dry.

-Hang the bunches of dill in upside down form, in a place that is dark, dry and warm. Ensure that the place has good circulation.

Harvesting broccoli

How do you know that your broccoli is ready for harvesting?

-Look at the head size. The broccoli head, typically, will get to around 4-7 inches wide when ready for harvesting.

-Assess the floret size. The individual sizes of florets or even flower buds are often the most reliable indicator. When the floret sizes reach the size of the head of a matchstick, get about harvesting your plant.

-Look at the color. Pay close attention to the floret color. The florets should be deep green in color. If you see a tinge of yellow, blooming is underway. Start harvesting immediately.

How to harvest broccoli

-Use a sharp knife and cut off the broccoli head off the plant.

-Make sure to cut off the broccoli head at least 5 inches or more below the head. Try to cut the head off with one swift cut and avoid sawing.

-After you harvest the main head, you may proceed with harvesting the side shoots of the broccoli. These will be growing as tiny heads to the side of where your main head was situated. By looking at floret size, it is easy to tell when your side shoots are ready for harvesting. Simply cut these off when they are ready for harvesting.

Part II: Dealing with weeds & common problems in companion planting gardening

Natural pest control in companion planting

No matter what pest you pick, there is always a natural control for it. Natural pest control is not only less expensive than purchasing and applying pesticides, it is also a lot safer for your garden and family. Since companion gardening is a potent tool for repelling pests from the garden, it is best to focus on how best to keep these pests from getting to your garden in the first place. This way, you have a complete protection package.

Prevention

The easiest way to prevent damage to your plants is by preventing the pests from coming in the first place. While it is true that companion planting acts as a great repellent to pests, this doesn't mean that companion gardening is pest proof. Pests can still cause considerable damage. So, how do you discourage pests from arriving in your garden in the first place?

Pull out any plants that appear weak

These plants may already be infected. If they are not infected, they may still draw predators to the garden. Pull the plant out and proceed to dispose it away from your area of gardening.

Build organic soil that is healthy

Natural methods of composting, mulching, and having your soil top dressed with natural fertilizer or compost are the surest way to develop strong plants.

Seaweed mulch

Seaweed has trace elements like zinc, iron, calcium, barium, magnesium, and sulfur. These elements will promote the healthy development of your plants. Seaweed fertilizer, either in spray or mulch form will enhance the growth of your plants and give them the strength to withstand diseases. The mulch of seaweed also works to repel slugs.

Minimize insect habitats

Clear your garden area of all debris and weeds, as these are breeding places for insects. You will also need to use clean mulch.

Rotate the crops in your indoor planting project

Insect pests are often plant specific. Companion planting is a potent tool to deal with pests. When you mix this up with active plant rotation, you will successfully avoid re-infestation of pests in your garden.

Keep the foliage dry

Be sure to water your plants early so that the foliage is dry for a better part of the day. Wet foliage will work to encourage fungal damage and insects to your plants. One of the best ways to irrigate your plants to ensure your foliage is dry is by using drip irrigation.

Disinfect your tools

If you happen to have been working on infested plants, clean your tools thoroughly before you move on to other garden areas. This works well to cut down on the speed of invasion by insects.

Weeds

Although companion gardening can help you to combat weeds, it might sometimes not be 100% weed proof. This makes it critical to use other methods to control weeds.

Weed control

Manual weeding is enough to control weeds. This simply entails using a fork and a trowel to get the job done making it very effective in a small garden. If you want to weed, the best time to do the weeding is during dry weather. However, ensure that you don't injure your crops while trying to remove the weeds. As a rule of thumb, ensure to get rid of the root systems otherwise you might end up fueling greater infestation.

Use weed killers

If you cannot remove the weeds manually, you can use foliage activated or soil activated weed killers depending on what you want. It is best to look for options that don't cause any harm to your plants; you don't want to cause harm to your flowers and or vegetables while trying to kill weeds.

Final tips

In as much as this book has done a great job of giving you tried and proven combinations, it is often a matter of trial and error. Still, following the tips and recommendations served in this book will vastly increase your success in pairing plants and watching them thrive together.

Follow these general tips and watch your garden transform:

*Beans do great with radishes

*Corns are great when paired with pumpkins

*Pair bean plants with radishes

*Pair your cabbages with beans

*Beetroot love broccoli. You cannot go wrong with this combination

*Plant lettuce and onions together

Conclusion

Thank you again for downloading this book!

Finally, if you enjoyed this book, please share your thoughts and post a review on Amazon.

Thank you and good luck!

PS: Can I Ask You A Quick Favor?

If you liked the book, please leave a nice review on Amazon! I´d absolutely love to hear your feedback. Every time I read your reviews... you make me smile. I´d be immensely thankful if you go to Amazon now and write down a quick line sharing with me your experience. I personally read ALL the reviews there, and I´m thrilled to hear your feedback and honest motivation. It´s what keeps me going, and helps me improve everyday =)

Please go Amazon Now and Drop A quick review sharing your experience !

***

THANKS!

***

ONCE YOU´RE BACK, FLIP THE PAGE!
BONUS CHAPTER AHEAD
=)

Check Out My Other Books

Are you ready to exceed your limits? Then pick a book from the one below. I can´t imagine anything more fun, fulfilling,and exciting!

http://www.amazon.com/Amanda-Johnson-B/e/B00W53B4GY/ref=ntt_athr_dp_pel_1

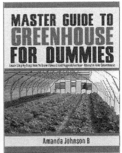

About the Author

They say a good gardener has a green thumb. If that's true, Amanda Johnson must have two green hands! Ever since she was a little girl, she loved spending time outside and helping her mother plant flowers each spring.

For her, the real thrill was in watching tiny seeds and bulbs transform into beautiful plants. As she grew, her hobby became her passion, and Amanda began helping friends and neighbors start their own gardens.

Today, she writes her tips, tricks, and expertise into easy-to-follow guides with the goal of doing her part in ma

Preview Of "Master Guide Green House"

Introduction

I want to thank you and congratulate you for downloading the book, *"Master Guide To Greenhouse for Dummies: Learn Step By Step How To Grow Flowers And Vegetables Year- Round In Your Greenhouse"*.

This has everything you need to have a thriving greenhouse.

Many of us who are into farming have one common wish; we would want to somehow provide a constant supply of fresh farm produce whether for sale or for our own consumption. However, one thing is pretty common in virtually every part of the world. This is the fact that the weather is constantly changing and that some plants might not do well in certain parts of the world due to different reasons like inappropriate heat or humidity or inappropriate soil that makes it almost impossible to grow whatever we want in the open field. So, does that mean that we should cut our losses and just wait for the proper season to grow whatever it is we want to grow? Well, not really. You can do something about the situation by providing the right conditions for whatever it is you are growing. The best way to achieve just that is through greenhouse farming.

A greenhouse can be a massive asset when you are growing veggies or starting seeds in your garden. It extends your growing season and will even go as far as providing you with fresh veggies through winter and even early spring. However, one thing to keep in mind is that successful veggie growing will require you to keep the right environment in the greenhouse. This book will teach you everything you need to know about greenhouse farming. So, let's get started.

Thanks again for downloading this book, I hope you enjoy it!

To start us off, we will talk about why you should give greenhouse gardening a try.

Why Opt For Greenhouse Gardening?

Greenhouse gardening is, in all honesty, the next level of gardening. Most gardeners know this well. Here are some benefits to help you decide if this advanced form of gardening is worth the money it asks you to spend.

Consistent, all year round gardening

With a greenhouse in place, it is a possibility to evade just about all the seasonal changes as well as weather conditions all year long. Long droughts, extreme temperatures and incessant rain will barely cause any problems to your efforts in greenhouse gardening. Try drawing a parallel with basic outdoor gardening and you are bound to see just how huge this is.

The planning of your garden shall no longer be dependent on the swings of the weather. What does this offer to you? Well, limitless flexibility with your gardening is just the start. Flexibility is what will make the difference between harvesting when everyone else is harvesting thus having to deal with a flooded market and harvesting when very few other farmers are harvesting. In this case, it helps you work around the issue of demand and supply for your crops thus making it possible to make more from your farm produce.

Superior Plant protection

Planting your plants in greenhouses will shield them from issues such as strong winds, rough weather, and serious seasonal infestation where pests are concerned. If a swarm of locusts comes to town and happens to pass over your outdoor garden with all its pretty greens, a lot of destruction just might be done. The same applies with Japanese beetles and spider mites. With greenhouse gardening, you simply watch the swarms pass by and wish them luck elsewhere.

Plants are extremely weak. Pests and rough weather will most probably kill them. Taking this into perspective, it is clear just how important greenhouse gardening is.

Optimum growing environment for your plants

If you are reading this book, chances are that you love gardening and know a thing or two about planting veggies and herbs. You probably know by now that plants, especially herbs and veggies, love warm, humid conditions and environments.

When you opt for greenhouse gardening, your plants will be placed under such a growing environment, easily enhancing their growth. Why is this? The main purpose a greenhouse serves is to secure a good amount of heat and water vapors to maintain the warmth and humidity within the greenhouse.

"No Season" Gardening

Perhaps, there was a time in the past when you were all excited about planting something in the garden only to realize that the season you were in was totally unsuited to the plant you wanted to plant. Usually, it is the temperature that factors in most of the time. Perhaps, you were able to wait for the amount of time it took and managed to hold onto your excitement. However, chances are that you probably never did what you wanted to do because the excitement had died out.

With a greenhouse, you have total control of the temperature of the garden. This will give you the power and ability to either plant before others or delay your planting activity. You have enough power in your hands to take both routes.

No need for landscaping

Landscaping is not an easy task, and it has never qualified as an easy job to carry out. Many aspiring gardeners tend to give up halfway through the process of landscaping either because the design is impractical or the whole procedure is simply too labor intensive or expensive.

If you take up greenhouse gardening, you can bid goodbye to all landscaping worries. Greenhouses, all of differing sizes and shapes laid out across your garden, will present a lovely exhibition, which ultimately is a great way to design the garden.

Now that you know how you stand to gain with a greenhouse, let's now get started to developing a functional greenhouse.

Important Tips With Regard To Setting Up Your Greenhouse

Part I: Important tips with regard to setting up your greenhouse

Starting your seeds

One of the most common uses of greenhouses is seed starting for both summer and winter gardens. With a greenhouse in place, it becomes possible for you to have an early start to your garden and even enjoy veggies all year round. The supplies you need for seed starting are sterile soil, containers, water, fertilizer and, especially for the northern gardener, ample heat and light.

One relatively inexpensive way to start your seeds is by using a propagation mat placed under seed flats. This will provide your soil with direct warmth, which in turn aids in the germination process. A good alternative to using seed flats is to sow your seeds directly into soil benches. So, how do you go about providing warmth? For starters, you can use a heat cable, dug in and buried approximately 6 inches in your soil.

Heating

Heating greenhouses is not as complex as most people make it out to be. If you have access to electric, natural gas, or even LP gas heaters, you should do just fine. Electric heaters are a favorite for greenhouse gardeners as they are considerably economical, flexible, as well as easy to install. The 240 volt heaters will generally provide more efficiency compared to the 120 volt kind.

However if your greenhouse is indeed quite small sized, the 120 volt heater will be adequate when under the control of a separately installed heavy duty thermostat that is moisture resistant. Make sure that your LP gas and natural gas heaters are adequately vented, with fresh air for combustion and exhaustion of fumes being easily available. Equip these with a solid thermostat.

Other less common methods of heating exist, with the inclusion of the in-the-floor radiant heating and an extension of a forced air heating system, to a greenhouse that is attached.

Lighting the greenhouse

Once your seeds come up, they will certainly need to do with some light. If your greenhouses natural light is low (for instance in the winter season), providing your plants with supplemental lighting will be necessary to keep them from growing spindly. Usually, a basic fluorescent light dangled around 4 inches above your plants will be enough. However, most gardeners will tend to go a step further and employ high output fluorescent lights, LED lights and metal halide lights. These lights will provide a powerful, full light spectrum and will often cover a larger area as compared to ordinary fluorescents. These lamps also double as incredibly energy efficient light sources.

Ventilation

When winter comes around, it will often be difficult to prevent mold and mildew from growing and establishing themselves. Do the best you can to avoid overwatering. The other thing to do is to make sure the greenhouse has proper ventilation and air circulation to help control the humidity within. For ample air circulation, install an oscillating fan that runs full time, all year long. As for ventilation, especially in the warmer months, the gentlest form of the same is via natural convection, with base wall vents and/or louvered windows. The windows pull in cool air down low, with the roof vents that allow hot air to leave through the roof.